READY, SET, DRAW!

SEA CREATURES
YOU CAN DRAW

Nicole Brecke

Patricia M. Stockland

Millbrook Press / Minneapolis

The images in this book are used with the permission of: © iStockphoto.com/Dzianis Miraniuk, p. 4;
© iStockphoto.com, pp. 4, 5; © iStockphoto.com/Boris Yankov, p. 5; © iStockphoto.com/JR Trice,
p. 5; © iStockphoto.com/Amanda Cotton, p. 7; © iStockphoto.com/Paul Wolf, p. 9; © iStockphoto.
com/Claes Torstensson, p. 11; © iStockphoto.com/Ian Scott, p. 15; © iStockphoto.com/Denis
Radovanovic, p. 19; © iStockphoto.com/Jaroslaw Brzychcy, p. 23; © iStockphoto.com/Kristian
Sekulic, p. 27; © iStockphoto.com/Nadezda Firsova, p. 31.

Front cover: © iStockphoto.com/Paul Wolf, (seascape); © iStockphoto.com/Denis Radovanovic,
(anemone); © Dorling Kindersley/Getty Images, (hand).

Edited by Mari Kesselring

Millbrook Press
A division of Lerner Publishing Group, Inc.
241 First Avenue North
Minneapolis, MN 55401 U.S.A.

Website address: www.lernerbooks.com

Library of Congress Cataloging-in-Publication Data

Brecke, Nicole.
    Sea creatures you can draw / by Nicole Brecke and Patricia M. Stockland ; illustrated by
Nicole Brecke.
      p.   cm. — (Ready, set, draw!)
    Includes index.
    ISBN: 978–0–7613–4168–0 (lib. bdg. : alk. paper)
    1. Marine animals in art—Juvenile literature. 2. Drawing—Technique—Juvenile literature.
I. Stockland, Patricia M. II. Title.
NC781.B74 2010
743.6—dc22   2009027090

Manufactured in the United States of America
1 – BP – 12/15/2009

TABLE OF CONTENTS

About This Book 4

Helpful Hints 5

How to Draw a STINGRAY 6

 How to Draw a KILLER WHALE 8

How to Draw a WALRUS 10

 How to Draw a GREAT HAMMERHEAD SHARK 12

How to Draw a CLOWN FISH 16

 How to Draw a BOTTLENOSE DOLPHIN 20

How to Draw a SEA TURTLE 24

 How to Draw a CRAB 28

Further Reading 32

Index 32

ABOUT THIS BOOK

Stingrays, clown fish, and crabs! These cool sea creatures really make a splash. With the help of this book, you can begin creating your own ocean friends. Draw a dolphin. Or sketch a sea turtle. Soon you'll know how to make many different sea creatures.

Follow these steps to create each sea creature. Each drawing begins with a basic form. The form is made up of a line and a shape or two. These lines and shapes will help you make your drawing the correct size.

A First, read all the steps and look at the pictures. Then use a pencil to lightly draw the line and shapes shown in RED. You will erase these lines later.

B Next, draw the lines shown in BLUE.

C Keep going! Once you have completed a step, the color of the line changes to BLACK. Follow the BLUE line until you're done.

WHAT YOU WILL NEED

PENCIL SHARPENER

COLORED PENCILS

HELPFUL HINTS

Be creative. Use your imagination. Read about great hammerhead sharks, killer whales, and walruses. Then follow the steps to sketch your own marine collection.

Practice drawing different lines and shapes. All your drawings will start with these.

ERASER

Use very light pencil lines when you are drawing.

Helpful tips and hints will offer you good ideas on making the most of your sketch.

PENCIL

Colors are exciting. Try to use a variety of shades. This will add value, or depth, to your finished drawings.

PAPER

Keep practicing, and have fun!

HOW TO DRAW A STINGRAY

The stingray hovers above the floor of the ocean. This clever creature both hides and hunts near sandy shores. The stingray's beady eyes sit on top of its flat body. But underneath are the animal's gills and mouth. Its mouth is full of sharp teeth. At the end of the stingray's long, skinny tail is a barb. The stingray can use this sharp spine to protect itself from enemies. The stingray uses electrical sensors in its body to locate prey, such as oysters and clams. Where does your stingray swim?

1 Lightly draw a base oval. Add a long, curved baseline.

2 Add another curving line to connect the left side of the baseline to the bottom of the oval. Draw a rounded V shape along the top of the oval.

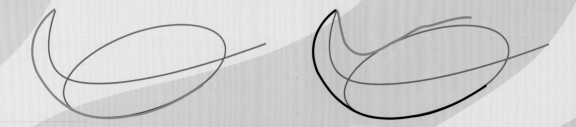

6

3 Make a pointy tail and a short line. Add a curved line behind the left fin. Draw a rounded triangle for the right fin.

4

Carefully erase your baseline and shape. Draw the head by making a flattened, open circle. Add two small eyes.

5 Now it's time to color your stingray!

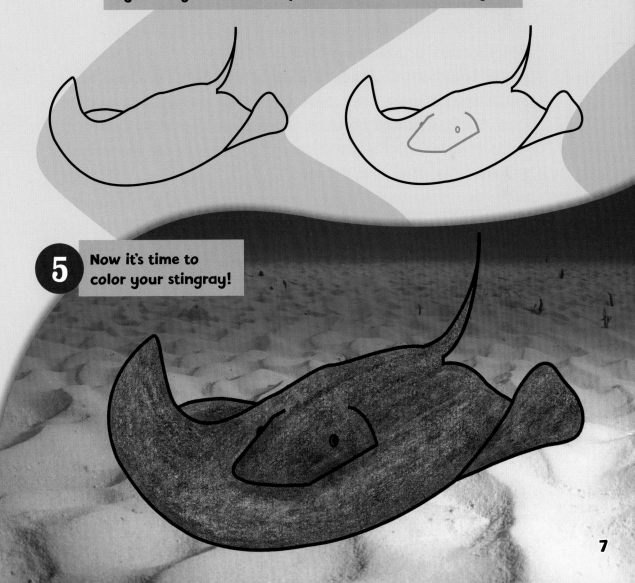

HOW TO DRAW A KILLER WHALE

The killer whale is no whale at all. Also called an orca, this black-and-white giant is the biggest of the dolphins. A killer whale can be nearly the length and weight of a school bus. The killer whale is supersmart too. Killer whales can communicate with one another through echolocation, or bouncing sounds off objects. Family groups called pods hunt together. In pods, killer whales are able to catch and kill more prey than they would alone. Pods hunt seals, squid, fish, and seabirds. Some killer whales live and perform in marine life parks. Scientists study these mammals to help killer whales in the wild.

1 Draw a thin base oval and curving baseline. Make a small curved line at the top of the oval. Add a dorsal fin and finish the back line.

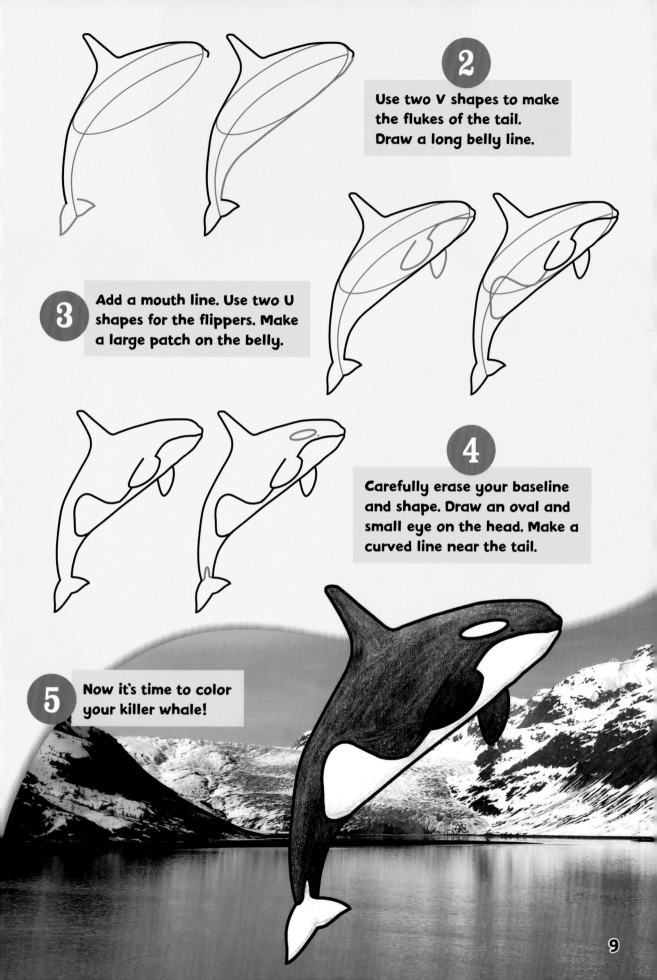

2

Use two V shapes to make the flukes of the tail. Draw a long belly line.

3 Add a mouth line. Use two U shapes for the flippers. Make a large patch on the belly.

4

Carefully erase your baseline and shape. Draw an oval and small eye on the head. Make a curved line near the tail.

5 Now it's time to color your killer whale!

9

HOW TO DRAW A WALRUS

The mighty walrus snorts and roars to its herd.
These huge creatures live in large social groups. A walrus
can be recognized by its long tusks, brown body, and beard
of whiskers. Both males and females have tusks. A walrus
uses its tusks in lots of ways, including to haul out (get out
of the water and onto an ice floe or beach). Large tusks
also help a walrus win fights with other walruses. Thick skin
protects a walrus during these fights. Blubber, or fat, keeps
the walrus warm in cold waters.

1 Draw a large base oval
and a smaller base oval.
Connect them with a
short baseline.

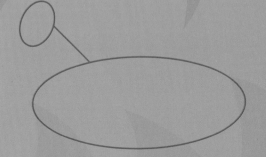

2 Use a rounded W shape to make the muzzle. Add a small curved
line under this and a longer curved line to complete the head. Draw
the chest. Add a long line with a bent end for the back and tail.

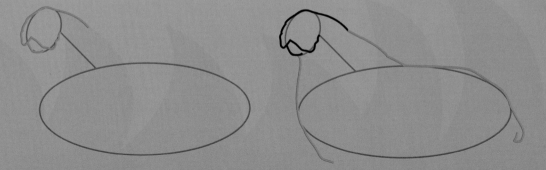

3 Draw a series of V shapes to create the front flippers. Make a larger back flipper. Add a line to complete the belly.

4 Carefully erase your baseline and shapes. Add two small nostrils and an eye. Use four vertical lines to create large tusks. Draw whiskers.

5 Now it's time to color your walrus!

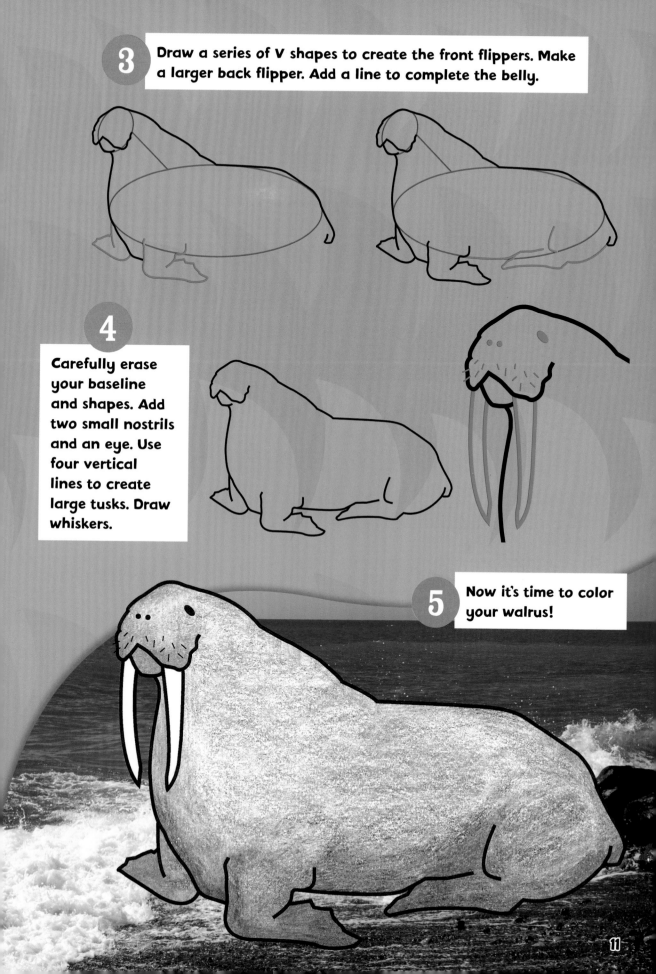

HOW TO DRAW A GREAT HAMMERHEAD SHARK

This powerful predator prowls the ocean in search of its favorite food: stingrays. Great hammerhead sharks are built right to trap the tricky rays. Sharks have an excellent sense of smell, which they can use to find food. The lateral line, a special system of cells along a shark's body, helps it sense movements in the water. The hammerhead can use its oddly shaped head to pin down a stingray. The great hammerhead also feeds on lobsters, squid, and small fish. This ocean hunter likes to stay in warmer waters such as those near coral reefs.

1 Draw a base oval. Add a curved baseline through the oval. Make a base rectangle at the bottom.

Inside the rectangle, draw a wide U shape and two horizontal lines. Add the back line and dorsal fin.

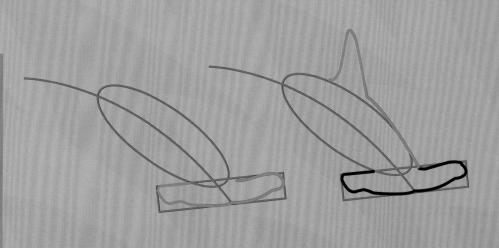

3

Finish the back line with a small fin. Make a large boomerang-shaped tail with a point.

4

Draw the underbelly with two smaller fins. Complete the belly line with another triangle-shaped fin.

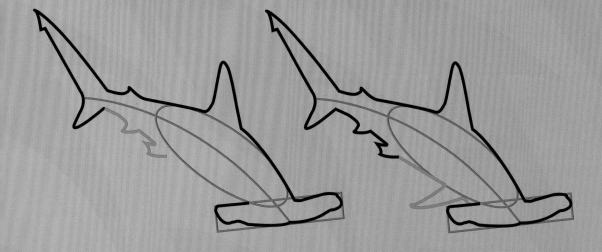

6 Add a large eye to each side of the head. Make three small lines for gills.

TIME TO EAT

Hammerheads love stingrays, but almost any fish will make a tasty meal.

DRAW A MACKEREL!

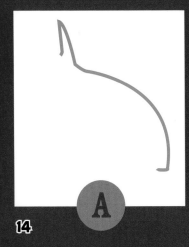

A

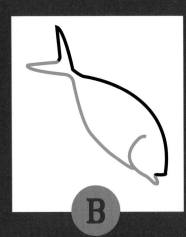

B

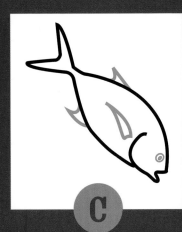

C

A great
hammerhead
shark can
be 20 feet
(6 meters) long.

7 Now it's time to color your
great hammerhead shark!

HOW TO DRAW A CLOWN FISH

The clown fish and the sea anemone make perfect partners. This colorful fish creates a symbiotic, or cooperative, relationship with an anemone. The clown fish keeps the anemone clean and healthy by eating parasites off it. The sea anemone protects the clown fish from enemies. The little clown fish can easily hide by swimming among the anemone's stinging tentacles. The clown fish is covered in slime, so it doesn't get stung. And it has another trick—changing from a male into a female. All clown fish are males at birth. Some become females as adults. Draw your own colorful clown fish!

1 Draw a base oval and a straight baseline. Add a **C** shape to the top.

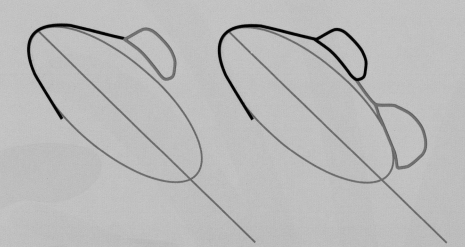

2

Make a flattened oval for the top fin. Add a short back line. Draw another slightly larger fin.

3

Draw the tail at the end of the baseline. Add another fin along the belly, and add a short curved line.

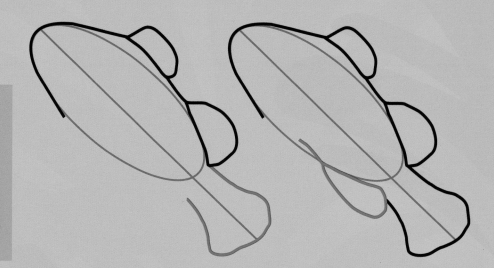

4

Make a rounded pair of fins at the center of the belly. Draw curved lines just inside each fin.

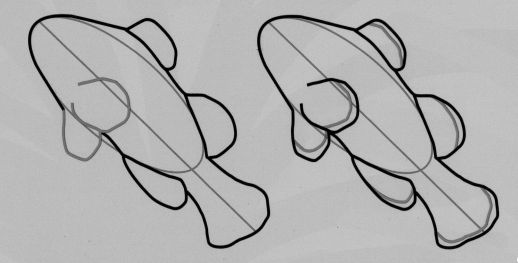

5 Carefully erase your baseline and shape.

6 Add a circle for the eye and two curved lines. Draw two more lines across the body and two near the tail.

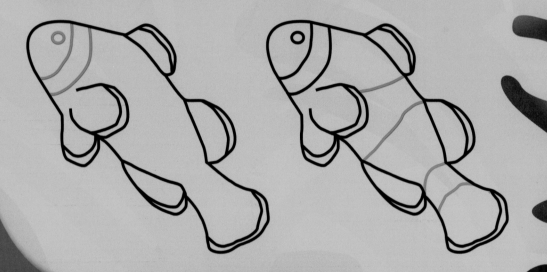

Did you know...

CLOWN FISH LIVE IN THE PACIFIC OCEAN AND THE INDIAN OCEAN AROUND AUSTRALIA AND INDONESIA.

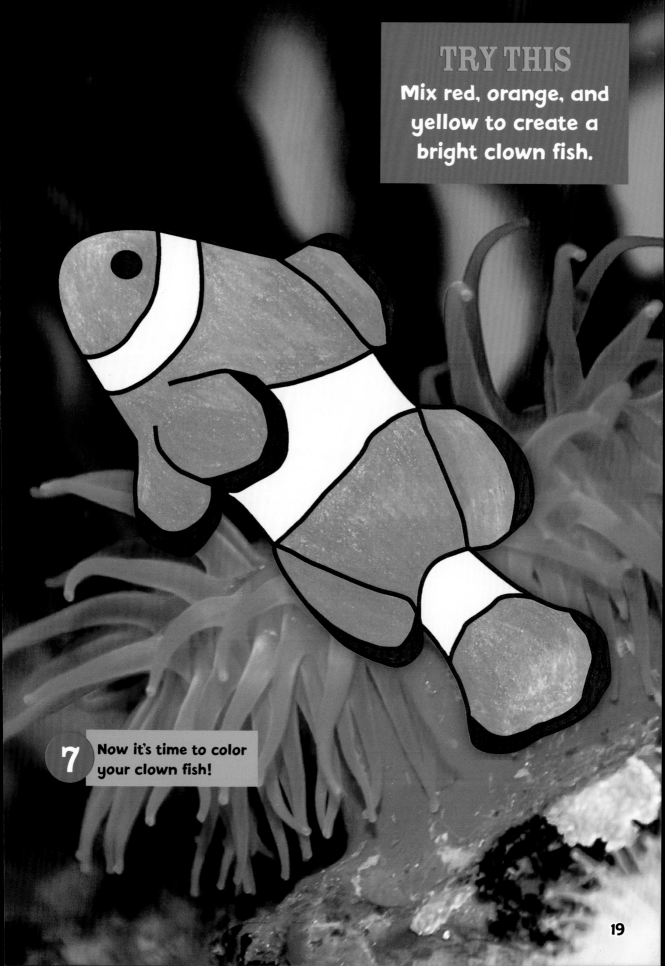

Mix red, orange, and yellow to create a bright clown fish.

7 Now it's time to color your clown fish!

HOW TO DRAW A
BOTTLENOSE DOLPHIN

Smart, smooth, fast, and friendly all describe the dolphin. Bottlenose dolphins are some of the best-recognized ocean mammals. One marine legend claims that dolphins bring good luck and clear skies to sailors. Dolphins can leap into the air, catch fish, and do other tricks. Some dolphins are trained to perform for a crowd. In the wild, dolphins are social creatures. They help one another hunt for squid, schools of mullet, and other fish. Through echolocation, they can find prey, follow boats, and communicate with one another. A group of dolphins is called a pod. Sometimes several pods swim and hunt together, creating large herds of hundreds of dolphins.

1 Draw a small base circle and a curved baseline. Add a base oval beside the circle.

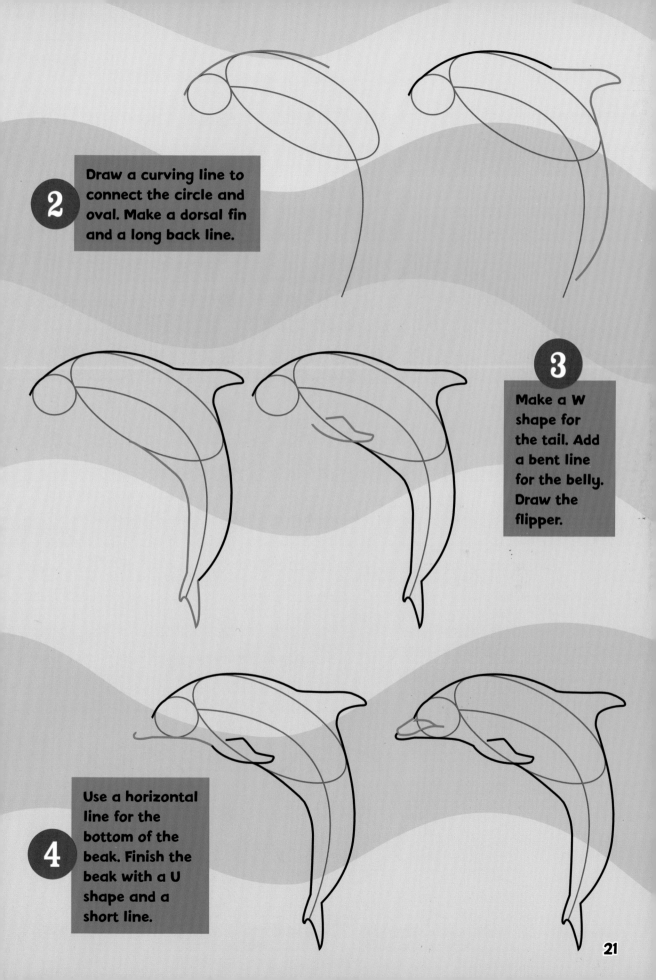

2 Draw a curving line to connect the circle and oval. Make a dorsal fin and a long back line.

3 Make a W shape for the tail. Add a bent line for the belly. Draw the flipper.

4 Use a horizontal line for the bottom of the beak. Finish the beak with a U shape and a short line.

5 Carefully erase your baseline and shapes.

6

Add a small oval for the eye and another for the blowhole. Draw a short line on the tail.

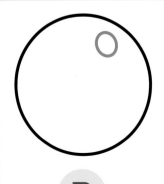

GAME
TIME

Whether in a show or in the open ocean, dolphins love to play.

DRAW A TOY!

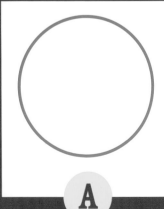

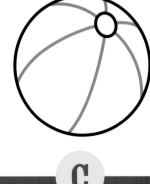

A　　　**B**　　　**C**

7 Now it's time to color your bottlenose dolphin!

TRY THIS
Use whites and silvers to make your dolphin look shiny.

A DOLPHIN breathes through its blowhole, which is on top of its melon, or head. Dolphins also have excellent eyesight and hearing.

23

SEA TURTLE

Sea turtles remain a bit of a mystery. These endangered (at risk of dying out) animals live in ocean waters around the world. Sea turtles are born on land. But males rarely come to shore after hatching. Females return to land only to lay their eggs. So it's difficult to count how many sea turtles remain in the wild. Still, these sea swimmers, which live most of their lives alone, continue to fascinate scientists. The leatherback sea turtle dives hundreds of feet to prey on jellyfish. The green sea turtle holds its breath underwater for hours. What can your sea turtle do?

1 Draw a base oval and a slightly curved baseline. Add a larger base oval.

3 Use two curving horizontal lines to draw the flipper. Add a bumpy diagonal line across the body.

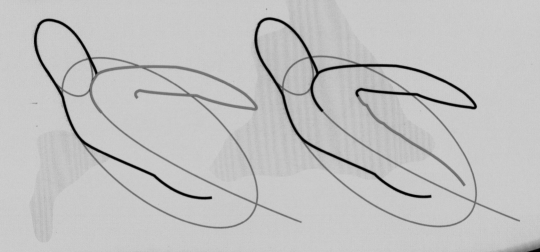

Fast Fact...
THE **CARAPACE** IS THE
TOP OF A **TURTLE'S SHELL.**
EACH TURTLE SPECIES
HAS ITS OWN **CARAPACE.**

4

Add two shorter diagonal lines. Draw two more slightly longer lines above these to complete the shell.

5

Make a larger back flipper. Add another back flipper. Use a V shape for the other front flipper.

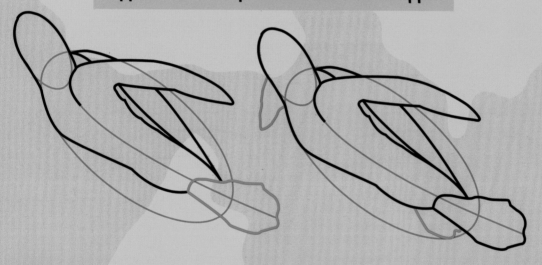

6 Carefully erase your baseline and shapes. Draw a curved line on the front flipper. Make a small eye, and add a curved line. Draw a small mouth.

SOME SEA TURTLES migrate, or travel, thousands of miles through the ocean. Then they return to their nesting grounds.

7

Now it's time to color your sea turtle!

TRY THIS
Use yellows, oranges, and browns to color your sea turtle.

HOW TO DRAW A CRAB

The crab isn't the friendliest of creatures. With powerful front pincers and a crabby attitude, this crustacean has a reputation as, well, a crab! But crabs are important. Different types of crabs can be found almost anywhere in the world's oceans and along its shorelines. Some live in the water. Others spend a lot of time on land. In the Atlantic Ocean, blue crabs help keep the food web in balance by eating fish, snails, plants, and even dead animals. Humans, in turn, hunt and eat crabs.

1 Draw a base rectangle. Add a horizontal baseline. Draw a base oval at each end of the baseline.

2 Make a bumpy rectangle inside the base rectangle. Add a horizontal line and two short vertical lines below this.

3 On top of each oval, draw a curved line. Add a W shape to the bottom of each. On each side, draw two bent lines to connect the pointed shape to the rectangle.

4 Make a curved line above the first pair of legs. Add a small triangle inside the curve. Complete the leg below the claw by making a pointed tip. Repeat this on the other side above and below the front leg. Add two more curves and two smaller points for the third pair of legs.

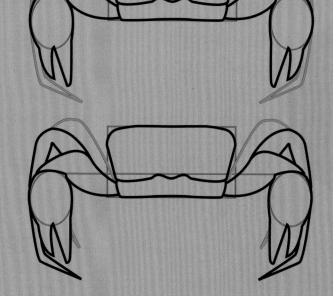

5 Add another set of shorter lines and points for the fourth set of legs. Finally, add the fifth set of legs.

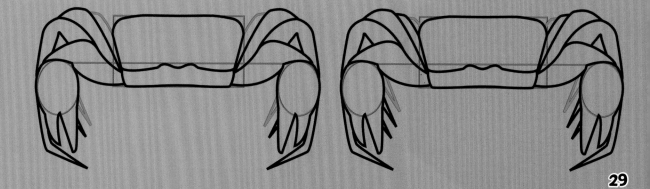

6 Carefully erase your baseline and shapes.

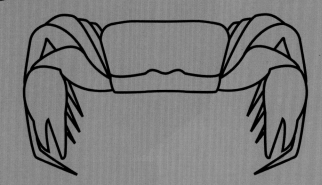

7

Draw two ovals for eyes. Add a smaller oval inside each larger oval. Connect the eyes to the body using short lines.

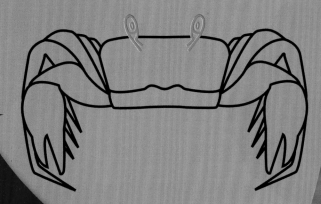

SWELL SHELL

Crabs aren't the only creatures on the beach. Mollusks and other shelled animals often wash ashore.

DRAW A SEASHELL!

A

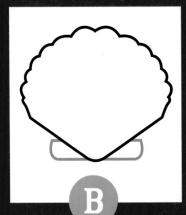

B

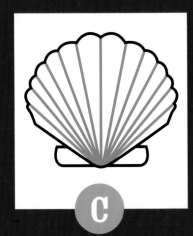

C

A blue crab's shell can be a mix of red, brown, and blue.

8 Now it's time to color your crab!

FURTHER READING

Booth, Jack. *The 10 Deadliest Sea Creatures*. Danbury, CT: Children's Press, 2007.

Davis, Buddy. *Sensational Sea Creatures*. Green Forest, AR: Master Books, 2005.

Jango-Cohen, Judith. *Real-Life Sea Monsters*. Minneapolis: Millbrook Press, 2008.

Monterey Bay Aquarium
http://www.montereybayaquarium.org

Schatz, Dennis. *Totally Sea Creatures*. San Diego: Silver Dolphin Books, 2003.

Secrets at Sea
http://www.secretsatsea.org

Secrets of the Ocean Realm
http://www.pbs.org/oceanrealm/index.html

INDEX

anemone, 16
Atlantic Ocean, 28

blue crab, 28, 31
bottlenose dolphin, 20–23

carapace, 25
clown fish, 16–19
coral reef, 12
crab, 28–31

echolocation, 8, 20

great hammerhead shark, 12–15

Indian Ocean, 18

killer whale, 8–9

lateral line, 12

mackerel, 14

Pacific Ocean, 18

seashell, 30
sea turtle, 24–27
stingray, 6–7, 12, 14

toy, 22

walrus, 10–11